A WALK IN THE GARDEN

A COLLECTION OF SPIRITUAL ANALOGIES AND TRUTHS

NANCY E. ALEXANDER

WESTBOW
PRESS®
A DIVISION OF THOMAS NELSON
& ZONDERVAN

WestBow Press books may be ordered through booksellers or by contacting:

WestBow Press
A Division of Thomas Nelson & Zondervan
1663 Liberty Drive
Bloomington, IN 47403
www.westbowpress.com
1 (866) 928-1240

ISBN: 978-1-5127-6129-0 (sc)
ISBN: 978-1-5127-6130-6 (e)

Print information available on the last page.

WestBow Press rev. date: 10/31/2016

CONTENTS

PREFACE

These thoughts and ideas traced their way across my mind so clearly and emphatically that I was compelled to record them as they came to me. As you contemplate these writings, I trust that you will find in them some meaning for your life as I have for mine.

Nancy Alexander

ACKNOWLEDGEMENTS

A Walk in the Garden has always impressed me as being God's gift. I am grateful to my son, David, and my daughter, Kay, for their vision and dedication to helping me publish it. My thanks go to Suzy Foster for helpful editorial suggestions. The insightful comments of the late Rev. Jo Carr were early and lasting encouragement to continue writing

All photographs in the book are by David Alexander.

INTRODUCTION

In the early 1970s, during a lay witness mission in my church, the final service was drawing to a close. As we sang, I closed my eyes. When I did, I saw a cross with an object below. Though the object was unknown, the cross spoke clearly. I was drawn to the altar, and at that moment, my life began to change. Years later, I would write regarding this experience:

> As I read Christian's experience in *Pilgrim's Progress* of his burden falling from his back and tears flowing at the sight of the cross with the sepulcher below, I had the calm assurance that God had spoken to me the same way that Sunday at the altar. And that in these past four years, he had been teaching me to accept what he gave me then— that indeed there is no burden that he has not taken from me. And when I have chosen to let these things for which I have concern or feel responsibility weigh heavily upon me,

I am saying to the Lord, "I don't accept what you have done for me."

A few weeks passed, and then one morning as I stood at the kitchen window gazing at the backyard, I suddenly said aloud, "I'll tell you what to do. I'll tell you what to say. I'll tell you what to do. I'll tell you what to say. I'll tell you what to do. I'll tell you what to say." While simple and clear, it would be years before these words would become a source of affirmation for the work created.

Following this experience, I began reading the Bible early each morning. One time, as I read, my eyes and interest left the page, and I began writing. Words came as quickly as I could write. For several years, I continued to write from time to time, with the words continuing to come without any real effort on my part to compose them. Although the words flowed freely, I do not recall being moved by their meaning.

In time, the inspirational thoughts diminished, and I eventually filed the writings, only looking at them occasionally. Thirty years after the last writing, I felt compelled one day to read them again. For the first time ever, I felt overcome with emotion as I read. It was as though I finally understood what I had written so long ago.

A Walk in the Garden

This walk begins as I find myself one day coming to a garden—a garden that seems to be surrounded by the world—a part of the world and yet set apart at the same time. I am here after wandering, with many others through life, and I wonder why I never found it before. How close might I have been without seeing it?

As I open the gate and step in, there is a man in charge of what seems to be going on here. The trees and plants are different from any I've seen before. There are people carrying baskets of fruit, but looking ahead, I see no fruit on the plants.

The man in charge gives me an empty basket and tells me that it is all I need. He gives no instructions about how to find the fruit or how to pick it. Instead, he says he will go with me as I move through the garden and tell me what to do.

Why the empty basket? If he is so different that he can be with all these people at once all over the garden, why can't he fill my basket and let me sit down and eat? It seems to me that would be just as easy for him and a lot better for me.

So we begin our walk. He tells me every step to take, where to turn, and when to start looking for fruit. I would much rather he gave me a map or a list of instructions. I find this a little irritating—being led around like this. But when I stop listening to him and decide to try on my own, I get lost. In fact, I don't have the information about which tree has the fruit that I need today, and he isn't passing out road maps … whether I like it or not.

We stop at a tree, but as I look up, I don't see any fruit. Still, he insists we climb it. And as we do, I begin to see the fruit hidden among the leaves or out on the end of a limb. But which is ripe? I've never seen this kind of fruit before. So again, I wait for him to tell me which to pick.

And he's right! It is the most satisfying food I've ever eaten. I wonder now why I hated letting him tell me how to find it. Surely next time, I won't be so independent.

So down from the tree we come. I thought I'd rest awhile after I ate. But that strange, satisfying fruit has given me quite an appetite suddenly, and I need to keep searching for more.

I think I can do it on my own this time. I remember exactly what we did to find the last fruit. So I'll be on my way. I would have thought he'd complain about my leaving him behind.

Suddenly I find myself among all these trees and plants, and I don't know which is which. Someone passes by with fruit in his basket, but when I ask him for some, it doesn't taste right to me, although this other person seems to be enjoying it.

So I wander around and climb a few trees searching for ripe fruit. I dig around in some berry vines, but to no avail. Finally, when I am hungry, scratched, and tired, I call out for him, and he's right there, speaking with me again and moving with me through the garden to find food.

In this walk with God, we experience distress and peace, joy and sorrow, discouragement and fulfillment—all these emotions at one point or another depending on the fruits we need and whether we respond eagerly or reluctantly to his love and guidance.

As we climb some of the more difficult trees, pull our muscles, and scratch our knees, it is his walking beside us, telling us each move to make (if we'll only listen and obey) that brings us to the ripe and satisfying fruit. This fruit not only makes us stronger and healthier for now, but also keeps us better prepared to climb the next tree that may bear better fruit that's harder to reach.

Then we begin to realize that no matter the circumstances of these climbs and searches (however difficult and unpleasant they are), his presences gives us courage and assurance to go on. We know that whatever we find (with his help) is the best possible thing we could have. We slowly begin to realize that he really loves us. Until we came to this garden, we had known something about love. We thought we had walked with people who helped us, gave us some good advice, and cared for us, and we were grateful. But we never knew someone who could go every step with us and make every climb with us, always bringing us to the thing we needed most. We did not know one with such patience who always waited for us while we learned how to make this walk with someone else leading us, how to take his hand and trust him, or how to change from being our own boss, as we had been outside the garden, to trusting someone else for decisions in our lives.

Even on the bad days, when we don't seem to be in tune with him or walk beside him, we know that we are still in his garden, and he is there. That assurance of his love and presence somehow outweighs the immediate circumstances that bring frustrations. We know that if we'll let him, he'll take our hands and move with us through those difficult situations.

4-14-74

APPLES

Reading the Bible is like eating an apple.

> Let's eat an apple! In fact, since we like them so much, let's eat a sackful! And when we finish, there we'll be—full of chopped apples, still red with the peel on them, same texture as before we started.

But that's not really the way it is at all. From the moment we eat the apples, they begin to change, becoming part of our bodies, contributing to good health. So if someone sees inside us later, they don't find apples; they see the results of the apples having been eaten.

As we read the Bible, if we read depending solely on ourselves to understand, we are only full of words. But if the Holy Spirit speaks to us through the words, he causes the meaning and truth that live in the words to penetrate our very lives so that we are not full of mere words, but the result of life-changing truth is reflected in us.

We should trust more and more in the Holy Spirit to speak to us as we read so that more and more of His truth will reach us.

But just as it is impossible to eat an apple and keep it in its original form, I wonder if it is impossible to continue reading the Bible without the Holy Spirit speaking through—perhaps even when we are not consciously aware of it. With each bit of truth that reaches us comes a bit of growth that contributes—along with other life-changing experiences—to making us the people God intends for us to be.

Just as the body, when functioning as it is designed to do, absorbs the food value that it needs, so the Holy Spirit sifts the words of the Bible, emphasizing what we need at the moment. With each reading, as our needs change, He speaks (often through words once passed over) to us where we are at that moment. There is no final, absolute interpretation of what the Bible says except in the truth that is God Himself.

4-16-74

The Little Things

God cares about everything that happens in our lives, whether it seems to us that these things would be important or unimportant to Him.

Nora dropped her earring (one she especially liked), and it rolled under the refrigerator. She got frustrated, because she didn't want to lose it, and she couldn't figure out how to get it. She also had extremely poor eyesight. She just sat down and prayed about it, and the thought occurred to her to use a yardstick; she did, and out it came.

Was she right? Did God answer a prayer about something as material and insignificant as an earring? Or did she just think about the answer herself? I believe He answered her prayer.

God created us to dwell and commune in fellowship with Him. The rest of creation is under our dominion. Its value and purpose lies in this relationship to us; it has no spiritual value to God except as it pleases and helps us. But God cares about us—our sorrows, joys, actions, attitudes, frustrations, everything. And if losing an earring frustrates us, God cares about it. He is concerned about our frustration.

When we pray, He'll act in some way (but we have to be open to His answer). It may not be to help us find what we want. It may be that the thought will come to us to use a yardstick; relax and try later; get Joe to help you; forget it, it's not that important; or something else. But if we respond *openly,* then the frustration will be gone. This, after all, is God's concern. The frustration is our concern, too, though we may not realize it. We may say, "God, I've lost my earring; what can I do?" but what we're really saying is, "God, I'm frustrated, and I need help. It may be stupid to be worried about such a trivial thing, but foolish or not, I am upset. Help me!"

This all started with Peggy's cat. We were discussing *Bone of His Bone* one Friday morning, and Peggy said she wanted to tell us about her cat—that God had answered her prayers. Then she told about how the cat had got caught in the garage door. Betty came by, and they had a terrible time freeing it, as it was rather mangled, and Peggy was confined to a wheelchair due to MS. Both Betty and Peggy got caught up in telling about it. This seemed somewhat trivial when we were trying to get into something as deep as the book we were discussing, but something told me that it was important to Peggy and Betty.

I thought about it later and wondered, "Does God answer prayers like this, or do some of us just believe He does?" Then it finally began to dawn on me that He loves us, and everything that happens to us matters to Him. His love and concern are centered in us regardless of where our love and concern are centered.

I don't remember what we were discussing in *Bone of His Bone* that day, but I'll never forget the cat.

4-74

BIRD IN FLIGHT

It is not so much that I am driven to know the truth, since no one can ever in this life completely understand and fathom truth or God. It is, rather, that I am compelled to know myself and see some meaningful and reasonable expression of where I am and what I believe about God and related things. And with each new thought or understanding, there follows a new or many new questions or leading thoughts. Is this an end in itself? Can this kind of venture and living make a person more able to relate to others in a helpful and meaningful way in their lives?

How do we find meaning in life, and how do we grasp truth? Where do we go to look for these things?

We might liken truth or this search for truth (which is a movement toward God, since God is truth) to a bird in flight. As we think about this bird, we see it being held aloft by an air current, but there is more than this to its flying. It is constantly moving from its present position to another just beyond, and on and on. So moving forward is required to keep the bird in the air. It has a destination that motivates it to keep moving and activates its flying ability. The bird does not just wish to be at its destination and immediately arrive; it must go through the flight, moving closer with each moment, coming closer but still short of where it finally will be.

So it is with truth. We cannot know this final, perfect truth and relationship with Him until some future point. As we move toward that point, we find ourselves at a certain place of understanding at any one moment. This position encompasses who we are in our relationship to God and what we understand of Him through our experiences with Him and the various ways He speaks to us. Our desire to know God, what He wants of us, and what this truth is in relationship to Him keeps us moving. As we move in the stream of His Spirit toward Him, our position is constantly changing, bringing us closer to Him.

Our position will not be a perfect one, and we cannot always know for certain whether what we believe is part of God's truth or something of ourselves. But as long as we respond to what God has revealed to us in His Word while wishing very much to do His will, we will ultimately know the truth, even if we stumble and fall and are wrong at times in the unfolding of this truth.

In order to trust the voice, prompting, or our understanding of God and know that we are not being deceived by our own desires, our experience must encompass a willingness to be surrendered to Him as best we can with His help; a belief that our view is God's will to the best of our comprehension; a willingness to let things, situations, decisions, etc. remain in His hands, regardless of the outcome; and a realization that even though it may not be the perfect decision or stance to take, God will see us through it and move us toward Himself, using even our mistakes to His glory when we leave all in His hands. Even in our weakness, God uses our willingness.

Just as there are certain factors that keep the bird in flight, we move toward truth one step at a time, propelled by acceptance of all of these things combined. Truth for us is only what God has revealed to us through His relationship with us, and it is through faith that we see it.

Before the bird has learned and is ready to fly, it will fall to the ground if turned loose in the sky. We will also fall as we find our own understanding and guidelines to be inadequate if we are not living in Christ. It is only in Him that we have the assurance of staying aloft.

If the bird closes its wings to stay aloft at one point, down it comes! So it is with us if we think that we can stop and rest everything in some discovered truth. If we feel that a certain truth can be the basis for living from now on, down we come!

We also need to be aware that we cannot fly for other people and that they cannot fly for us. We may help each other as we observe, are observed, and relate to each other, but we can never comprehend completely the exact stance and position of another. We do not know exactly what God is saying to that person or the purpose God has outlined for him or her.

When a person meets God and surrenders to Him, the Holy Spirit will guide that person into truth. If we surrender our lives to Him, He has His own way of communicating with us and will make Himself known to us. It is this communication that we must follow, no matter how faint or ridiculous it seems. It is the only thing we can follow.

The reality of flight for the bird is just where it is at that moment. Its position is dependable only if it depends on its present condition while yielding to things that propel it forward. The reality of truth is just where we are at any given moment. It is dependable only if we are doing things that propel us forward.

The truth within ourselves is the part of God that He has revealed to us.

5-18-74

The Ferris Wheel

The Ferris wheel always frightened me. I had enough faith in it to believe it was well built and strong enough to hold me up and not fall, but when I got on, I took anxiety with me—as if my anxiety could influence what the Ferris wheel was going to do. And as a result, I was frightened, even though I was safe. But others obviously were able to trust it and get on without fear. They completely relaxed (resting, not just sitting) and totally enjoyed the ride even though they were taking the same ride and experiencing the same circumstances. They actually enjoyed the experience of what the Ferris wheel was designed to do for them.

Sometimes we have faith in Christ, but we find ourselves trusting our own ability to maintain faith instead of trusting Christ. When things go wrong, we become anxious about our faith, begin trying to find it again, and regain some experience of faith. We have faith that is not totally in

Christ and speaks, to a degree, of our own efforts to maintain this faith.

The Bible says we are one in Christ. This is expressed in the sixteenth chapter of the Gospel of John by the analogy of the vine and branches. So faith moves beyond trusting in Christ and also rests in Christ.

We are a part of Christ so completely when we accept this completed gift of grace that there is nothing we can do beyond that point of initial faith. Faith is no longer something to be exercised (in the sense of faith moving from us to Christ). It is, instead, a state of being in Christ that He maintains. We completely rest in this state without anxiety, question, or effort. He lives through us and directs our concerns and efforts toward serving others.

This does not make us perfect; however, we are being perfected in Christ. While He reaches others through us, the self is submerged. The Holy Spirit will still cleanse and sanctify us, but this will be secondary to His other work in and through us. We pass the point of any anxiety about our salvation, because if we rest in Christ, He assumes *all* the responsibility. We are totally free to be used by Him as He chooses.

5-24-74

HEBREWS 11:1

"Now faith is the substance of things hoped for, the evidence of things not seen."

Faith in God takes the long view of life, assured that regardless of circumstances God will be victorious.

Faith is knowing that God has the answer and will manifest it. We must be willing to trust His judgment, knowing that it is best for us whether we understand it or not. We must trust without reservation so that the right thing (God's way) is assumed to be already a reality (even though, perhaps, it is yet to be). It must be substantive, and we must live in light of this assumption.

Faith is looking into the face of God with all else on the periphery of our vision. As this faith becomes a reality for us, He sends us back into the "all else" of life. But this time, we take Him with us.

10-14-74

The Scholar

The Christian's life is like an experience in a classroom. God starts with him when he is just as the first-grader who begins school, only one day ahead of where he was the day before he started. He brings himself to that first day of school but is not the scholar he will one day be.

Then gradually, as he is exposed to teaching, day after day, year after year, he changes intellectually. Although he will move along with a group his own age as a body that is identified with a certain level, his intellect is unique. With every bit of learning, there is a unique individual response from the student to the given challenges.

The learning that takes place is always dependent on how well he understood the previous lesson. If he has only been filling his head with facts instead of learning in such a way that really changes his thought processes, then there is little stability in his position, and he may easily become confused.

For instance, if he doesn't really know how to add one column of figures and understand what he's doing, when he starts to add two columns, he may be able to get the right answer by memorizing the process but will always be one step away from confusion, because the technique is not actually his. The more difficult the problems become, the more slippery his footing will be, until finally, he will no longer be able to cope. Then the only thing for him to do will be to go back to the one-column problem where he started and move at his own pace, not that of the person sitting next to him.

God works with the Christian in the same way. He begins with the surrendered life—just where it is—and starts the lessons. Every person will not have the same first lesson, because God knows the heart and life of each of us and the exact next step needed to make us what He wants us to be.

Before God challenges us with the second lesson, He makes the first technique or knowledge a real part of us; we live it through. This lesson gives us strength that supplies our capacity to live through the next lesson He has for us.

It is very important not to move ahead of the teacher in our excitement over the discovery of a new truth. There are certain steps that must be taken to reach the next truth because of who and where we are. If we overestimate our intelligence and grab for the next truth, avoiding the tedious learning in the steps that lead to the truth, then we find ourselves holding an answer that has no meaning for us.

Avoiding the learning steps is like looking in the back of the book for the answer to the math problem. We can get by with it if we only need to repeat an answer and never need to understand the process by which the answer was reached.

But when life really shakes us up, repeating someone else's answer doesn't help much. We must learn the process for ourselves. It is very true that we often learn by observing others, and what is most helpful is seeing how their learning process is applicable to us. We can't live on someone else's answers or commitment.

We may move along in the shadow of others and feel a certain security if we have no problems that seem to overpower us. Since no one is perfect, we must put our ultimate faith and trust in God first, or we will ultimately be lost on the wrong path.

10-26-74

The Tomb

We may take Jesus, wrap Him in the knowledge we have acquired about Him, place Him on a shelf with plans to care for His body, and go to visit when we want to be near Him. Then later, when we go to pay our respects, we wrestle with the huge stone, easing it aside just enough to see into the darkness of the tomb, imagining that we see Him there in the linens. Satisfied, we close it again, not to return until we feel a pang of loneliness or regret or sense a special need to see Him and know where He is.

We can be deceived by our own desire to control our lives. Our plans are all made. We have found our place. Our family fits next to us, we fit our friends in here, our business goes there ... success has a spot. To the side, in the dark, we put Jesus, all wrapped up. When we want to see Him, He'll be easy to find.

But until we take a good look, we only mislead ourselves. Christ cannot be contained in such a place. All we have are the linens in which we wrapped Him and the shelf on which we laid Him. The tomb in which we placed Him is empty.

Then one day, as we pay a respectful visit, a ray of light shines past the corner of the slightly opened stone. At the sight of the empty grave clothes, we're shocked and frightened and have an impulse to close it quickly. Suddenly, we know things aren't as we thought they were. Do we really want to see what's there? How can we control Him when we can't find Him? All that time, we thought we knew where He was.

The ray of light coming from outside the tomb is Christ Himself. If we just open that stone, He'll flood the darkness with His brilliance. And as we start to roll the stone away, we'll find Him doing that for us also.

He changes our relationship with Him from a false concept we had to a true life with Him. He floods the tomb with light!

The glory of Christ is not what we do with Him but what He does for us.

10-29-74

Moment of Truth

When God is working in our lives, there will be times when even though we know He is with us, the pieces just won't fit together. We may experience answered prayer, hear inspirational words from a friend, suddenly have a meaningful thought, understand what some writer is saying—yet the pieces won't really fit together. It's like an assembly line. Each station seems right, and its component is complete, but we don't see any final product that seems to have real purpose.

Suddenly, when we come to the right place—the end of the assembly line—all the pieces fall into place. We see fragments of things that happened become a part of an awareness or truth that God has been teaching us.

This moment of truth may come through various means. It often comes through the witness of another who had a similar experience or learned a similar lesson and has already passed this moment of truth. This person has seen the light so vividly that he or she is able and eager to pass it on. As we listen to that person, God works through that person and us to fit the pieces together to form the picture He wants us to see. Three things come together—our experience, another's witness, and the power of the Holy Spirit.

Some of the things we believed were happening but still had no assurance of are verified as truth, as we see them find their place in the completed product. We are filled with joy as we hear God say to us, "You can trust me. You must have faith and keep moving with me even when you don't see the purpose. I will reveal to you enough along the way so that you will be assured that I am with you. I will teach you to know my voice."

10-74

The Kingdom of God

In the thirteenth chapter of Matthew, we find a variety of descriptions and analogies of the kingdom of God. These parables suggest that the ever-present, living God is available but not containable. There is always something more of Him to be received, to be understood.

Attempting to capture the essence of the kingdom of God is like trying to paint a picture of the ocean with the intent of saying, "The ocean always looks exactly like this." The instant we start to paint, the waves roll, and with each stroke of the brush, it is the same. It would be impossible to paint an exact picture, because the ocean is in constant motion, and whatever we paint would not remain absolutely true. It would be simple enough to paint a picture of a dead sea with stagnant, motionless water. What we would paint one minute would still be true the next minute. But there is no life.

God did not reveal Himself once and then sit back, inactive, and wait to be found, understood, analyzed, and absorbed into our lives. If this were so, we would be able to know Him in His fullness, and our God would be much too small. God is living, moving among us, revealing Himself.

This opens a whole new world that is available to each of us. It is not a world of words and events from the past that are only to be imprinted on our minds with hopes that our intellect and reasoning will bring us some enlightenment. It is not simply truth that sits quietly as we decide what to do with it. No, it is a new world that offers a daily walk with the *Word* that is spoken fresh and new each day. Though our eyes follow the same words that have been read for centuries, the meaning that reaches our minds (if we are committed to Him and seeking His way) is His Word for us that moment as we read—a Word direct from God that has in it such truth that it rolls as the waves roll but never loses its essence or reality.

12-18-74

SALVATION

Salvation is both a present reality and a potential process as we receive Christ and He comes to dwell in us, bringing with Him all that He is— dead, resurrected, ascended. We live out this potential with its changing into reality in us. We live in time so far as the world is concerned and yet are completed with God in His eyes.

This truth regarding salvation is also seen in creation. We understand that within creation, there is infinite potential. We create nothing ourselves but only discover what God has placed here. So in a sense, creation is complete in God's eyes, although to the world, bound in time, it seems incomplete, since new discoveries are always being made that open new avenues.

In God's eyes, we are saved through Christ eternally. In this life, we live out our salvation by the Holy Spirit's direction.

So we are recreated in Christ just as we have been created in this world and as a part of this world—a creation both complete and to be completed.

12-26-74

THE MASTER PLAN

God's plan is like a tapestry that He is constantly weaving, using available threads. When we first believe, He ties in the thread at the outer edge of the picture. We may just want to dangle there a while—we're happy to be tied on; it seems enough for us. God wants to move us into the picture, but our tension isn't right to yield to His hands.

Finally, we let Him move us one day. He picks up the thread and goes up the back of the tapestry, all the time creating a beautiful picture on the front. We begin to wonder what's out there in front—all those other threads are going in and out, some staying in front for a long time. Why doesn't He take us out there? After all, we're just as good as the next thread.

What we don't know is God's plan for the picture. We may have some ideas. We have seen some of the colors He uses, but even those who go through are so close to the picture that they can't see the overall scene, only their surrounding area. Since we are a certain color, we don't know when or where our color fits in. It may be that we only fill a small spot, or maybe there is a larger space for us that comes later. It's God's plan, and He knows.

We get tired of waiting and decide to go through and be a part of things. When we do, we move against the balanced tension with which God holds us, dart through the tapestry, and pop our thread. We are out front, like we wanted to be, but all frayed out.

The wonderful thing about God is that when we relax again and realize we have goofed and the tension gives, He can begin to work with us again. He'll gently pull us back through, tie us together, and continue to use us where He needs us.

Then maybe one day, He wants to carry us through and use us out front. Now we don't feel like going. We've never been out, and we're afraid. What if He thinks He wants us, we get out there, and we're not the right color? Does He know what He is doing? We don't want to be a part of a picture we can't see completely. We'd like to see the picture He's making and then decide if we want to be in it.

When He starts to move us through, we balk and tighten up. He won't force us. Instead of the picture that He might have made using us at this particular spot, in His miraculous way, He keeps the picture moving, using those who will be used as He needs them, adjusting somehow for those who won't (using them later, perhaps, if they'll let Him), but always weaving a picture that is His—a product of His mind that constitutes His plan. He does not change His picture for us but only seeks to bring us into it, working with patience and long-suffering.

Our prayers, wills, and good intentions—none of these things change the mind of God or His plan. We either come to be a part of it as He conceives it, or we are not in it.

Even our refusal to be used as He wishes does not change His plan, for ultimately, He is always looking toward a completed plan conceivable only to Him. He has all the time He needs, and He's in charge!

1974

Feeding Time

John Wesley said, "If your heart is as mine, give me your hand." What a beautiful philosophy—but how difficult to practice

Our confusion, irritation, and obsession with the differences in manner of worship of various denominations and religious groups is similar to the confusion that might well exist in the farmer's barnyard.

At feeding time, the farmer goes out to the barnyard and finds his cows, horses, pigs, chickens, rabbits, and sheep waiting for him. To the pigs, he gives one kind of food—scraps from the kitchen. The chickens take a mixture of grain; the horses seem very well satisfied with hard ears of corn, and so on. Each creature is happy with the food the farmer gives, for he obviously knows what is best for each animal.

But as the chickens finish their meal, for the first time they take a look around them. They suddenly begin to laugh hysterically; the pig has just eaten his scraps and is going to sleep in perfect contentment. "What a fool! Doesn't he know that he couldn't possibly be that content? Only chicken feed satisfies the appetite.

"And that sheep—who does he think he is? Such a snob! He grazes around the pasture on that short, stubby grass and then comes in here with us and just looks. He doesn't know what he's missing. I wonder how I could convince him that he needs some of this chicken feed?

"See that fat, healthy-looking cow over there, munching on the hay? Poor thing; she doesn't realize she's half-dead. She really couldn't be serving any good purpose. Makes me wonder if the farmer really knows what he's doing. Shouldn't he throw the poor cow a little chicken feed? I personally know from experience that it's the *only* food."

1-76

BURDENS

As I read Christian's experience in Pilgrim's Progress of his burden falling from his back and tears flowing at the sight of the cross with the sepulcher below, I had the calm assurance that God had spoken the same thing to me that Sunday at the altar. In these past four years, He has been teaching me what He gave to me then. Indeed, there is *no* burden that He has not taken from me. And when I have chosen to let those things for which I have concern or feel responsibility weigh heavily upon me, I am saying to the Lord, "I *don't accept* what you have done for me."

When our eyes are on the cross, all burdens fall from us into the open sepulcher, and we are free—free to love God, worship Him, and do His will. Then He lives in us and through us so that as we live and move in His will, we are instruments that meet the needs of the world around us. With His work through us, concerns and responsibilities are met and seen—not as overpowering burdens but opportunities and avenues for His love to be manifest in real, life-changing ways.

2-1-76

One Truth

There is one truth—God. All things that have been, are, or will be live out that truth. There can be no deviation from it, for everything lives and has its being in relation to this truth. Nothing breaks outside the realm and control of God. We are either in tune with Him or alien to Him; but whatever our position, He is over all. We do not escape His truth by turning our backs on Him. If we deny Him and cling to ourselves, we have not created a kingdom of our own but have only fallen into a state of separation from Him, over which He has already won the victory.

We never escape His presence; we only refuse to acknowledge it. The gift of life is always available. We have to turn loose the self and receive Him with empty hands and hearts.

Spring 1976

ENDLESS LOVE

There is nothing more devastating than the despair that comes with the realization that we have alienated the one we love. An aching hunger tells us that the relationship is gone, and the love we would have once received from our loved one is no longer available.

The awareness gradually dawns on us that when the love was there, we took it for granted, were much too sure of ourselves, and felt somehow that nothing could threaten this relationship.

Peter must have anguished over his denial of his Lord. He had been so secure those years they had been together. Certainly, there were doubts and misunderstandings—days when he knew he wasn't living up to the standards Jesus seemed to direct him toward. But as he stumbled along, Jesus was always close by with His open heart, compassion, and patience. Yes, Peter was growing stronger and stronger! When the tension began to build in the little group and circumstances became more threatening, he was more sure than ever that no matter what happened, he would stand tall as someone his Lord could be proud of.

The fears mounted and before he knew what he'd done, out it came— the brash denial. From deep inside him, it broke to the surface. It was almost as if he heard another speak the words—someone he didn't even know who was unlike the man Peter thought he had become.

But it was done—too late now to stop it. The heavy burden of guilt poured upon him, smothering all other thoughts and feelings. *Why, oh, why did I do it?*

There is no desire like the desire for one you feel is gone forever. There is no repentance like that which pours out when there seems to be no listening ear or hope for redemption. Peter had turned his back on the Lord. No one would have blamed him—at least, no one who could have stood in his shoes that night. But the conviction was there, deep inside. Peter knew he was guilty, and for the first time, Jesus wasn't there to help him.

Though Peter was unaware of it, God never left him. He was there with His love, gradually, in His own time, making Peter into the person He knew Peter could be. We are never more able to receive the grace and power of the Lord than when we are utterly empty of pride.

When God's love comes pouring in, taking the guilt away, our relationship is stronger than ever—not because He has changed, but because He has changed us. There is a new dimension to our surrender to Him. The way is open for His power to flow more joyfully through our lives.

The dark and bitter experience has been transformed by the all-encompassing *love of God.*

8-21-76

The Narrow Way

Jesus said, "I am the Way." We are at other times reminded that the way is narrow. How narrow? If so many of differing faiths and practices are so assured they have found the way, why does there seem to be so much difference in their professions? Who is right? There is only one way and yet so many ways.

Our relationship to God as expressed in a way is analogous to our relationship to the sun as expressed in a direct line. If at high noon, we were asked to show someone the sun, our arms would go straight over our heads. There could be no question that this was indeed the only straight line from us to the sun.

But at this same moment, a person to the west, when asked to point to the sun, would hold his arm forward from his body at a ninety-degree angle, totally assured that this was the straight line from him to the sun.

Is the sun so undependable? Are people so wrong in their awareness of where the sun is? It seems that the manner in which they point to the sun depends on where they stand in relation to the sun. As they point to the sun at any one time, they must do so from their current position. It would be a little foolish for a person to imagine that he or she was standing with a friend six hours away and point as the friend is no doubt pointing. A person must see the sun as it is revealed to him or her.

God comes to us wherever we are. He does not ask us to stand in another's place and see Him through another's position or pretend that another's experience is ours. He asks us to look straight to Him as best we can considering our ability to see. No matter where this line is or how strange it looks when compared to that of others, if it is the straight line from us to God, it is the right way for us.

The straight line from a person to God is the narrow way. This narrow way is Jesus, for Jesus is God's gift to us—our companion on the way and the only way to God. Through Him, God comes to us, gently leading and shaping us into what He wants us to be. He is the initiator. He knows best the growth and experiences we need, for He alone is all-knowing.

8-27-76

PERCEPTIONS

Imagine a gathering of the followers of Jesus in AD 40. They have come together to praise Him and reflect on His great goodness. Excitement fills the air as they begin to share some of their experiences from the past few years.

With great enthusiasm a follower begins "I shall never forget the day! There I was, snugly perched in the tree. I just wanted to get a good look at Him. It never occurred to me that He'd ever notice me there. 'Come down!' And before I knew it, we were eating together at my table. How He changed my life! I am so glad I climbed up in that tree."

"What an interesting story, my friend, but rest assured, the most meaningful experience one can have is in the synagogue. From birth, mind you ... from birth, my hand was crippled. And in a moment, He looked at me with those compassionate eyes and spoke words that brought healing. I often wonder what would have happened to me by now if I had not been in the Lord's house that day.

I cannot believe that a chance encounter at a tree could have the same impact."

"That's all very well, but I think there was something magic in His touch—even the clothes He wore. I only touched the hem of His garment and was made whole … not a word spoken until after the healing. Don't tell me of synagogues and trees. I *know* how to have the greatest experience of a lifetime."

As one after another of Jesus' followers relates his or her personal story, each so sure that his or hers is the right one, coolness begins to fill the air. The excitement and joy on their faces gradually give way to doubt and frustration. Indeed, they have discovered that the Lord is not the greatest thing in their lives. Much more important is the manner in which He spoke to them and the method that He used.

12-2-76

The Seed

I believe that God wants us to work and take responsibility in life; we have a place in his divine purpose. However, we cannot assume creative functions that are His alone.

The farmer labors long hours, planting and nurturing the seed. His attentions, if in tune with the seed's character, will enhance its growth; if adverse, his actions will be damaging. He has learned to not only care for the seed because he wants it to grow, but also recognize a greater power than himself at work in its development. This knowledge has made him willing to follow the procedure that will bring maturity, and he is patient in learning what that procedure is.

Much like the farmer, we must acknowledge that some facets of life are beyond our understanding and control. Often, the results of our endeavors will be related to the possibilities inherent in a situation. God, who alone knows the true nature of His creation, calls us to yield our will to His so that our divinely inspired efforts can be transforming.

5-7-77

MY CREED

Yes, I have a creed. And I would share it if it were more easily defined.

A study of the Apostles' Creed, the Nicene Creed, and other meaningful expressions of the Christian faith offers theological insight, but the creed that is legitimately mine emits from my own experiences—my relationship with God, other people, and all of life.

The search for a better understanding of my Christian creed will continue. Perhaps the quest will open avenues of God's truth that I have not known.

August 1977

FELLOWSHIP OF THE UNSEEN

As I strolled around the deserted campus with my daughter, a silent presence made itself known. Though only our footsteps were heard, I sensed that others walked with us in warm fellowship.

Or was my imagination playing tricks? Were the old stone buildings, stained glass, and artifacts from around the world calling forth a response to their own interest and beauty?

The words of the writer to the Hebrews came to mind: "Therefore, since we are surrounded by so great a cloud of witnesses, let us also lay aside every weight and sin which clings so closely, and let us run with perseverance the race that is set before us" (Hebrews 12:1).

I knew that long after the impressive buildings were gone, the spiritual presence would still be there, embodied in a greater one who tenderly envelops us wherever we are. He has promised that He will never leave us, and surely those who follow Him remain a part of His spirit down through the ages, inspiring others as they answer His call.

6-78

This was written following my first visit to Scarritt College with daughter, Kay Beth, who was returning for the summer semester.

MIRACLES

Things that seem miraculous to us are surely not miracles to God, who sees all from a different perspective—a perspective of total truth.

No matter how difficult a situation, there lies within it the created possibility of perfection waiting to be realized. Just as in the beginning, He created the heavens and the earth from darkness and void, He continues his glorious creation, calling forth all things to fulfillment.

8-12-78

The Secret Place

The heart is a secret place. As I live within my own, I cannot help but wonder if there are other people who see life as I see it, understand God exactly as I understand Him, and have the same experiences with Him as I have.

If I can never know, the responsibility of my experiences weighs heavily upon me. Has another heard His voice in the same way I have heard it? Does He speak to others the things I hear Him speaking to me? Or does He depend on me to share a revelation that is uniquely mine?

I think I shall never know for certain, since the secret place of another is not open to me. I must assume that God has given me something that must necessarily be shared if His purpose is to be fulfilled.

11-78

OUR UNIQUENESS

When I meet thoughts, ideas, questions, or circumstances, I bring a unique background, experience, personality, and temperament unlike that of any other. My response to these life situations must be made in light of my understanding of God's will for me. The stances and experiences of others are often valuable aids, but they must never be my standard. Only God knows perfectly the proper actions needed for me to reach my potential.

In this sense, from our point of observation, we all march to a different drummer, for the sounds we each hear will never be quite the same. But in reality, it is the same drummer playing the rhythm for each of us that will put us in step and in tune with our Creator and in harmony with life around us.

5-7-79

FLEXIBILITY

I have heard it said that we should keep an open mind, at least consider new ideas, whether or not we adopt them. Can we take this advice while holding strong convictions?

As her friend pointed toward the tree, Maria caught her first glimpse of an apple. But the lush green leaves blocked her view, revealing only the short stem. For Maria, an apple appeared, at that moment, to be a brown twig.

Later, in the library, her concept expanded when she saw the fruit behind a low stack of books. The lower half of the apple was hidden from her sight. Then she knew it was very flat on the bottom with a rounded top and a bright red cover. She recognized the apple by its stem.

Reaching out to take it in her hand, she discovered its true shape. Her surprises had only begun. She had yet to observe its inner texture, to wonder at the small seeds resting in its center, or delight in its tangy sweet taste.

Isn't our relationship with God and our understanding of His ways similar to Maria's experience with the apple?

As we respond to life with a degree of flexibility rooted in a solid base, the way is open for clearer revelation of God's truth.

An apple can appear to be a short brown twig, but it is considerably more.

6-79

GRACE

Lord, I am so tired…
I am tired of going there day after day,
    even though I know I'm needed and it's something you
    want me to do.
I am tired from the guilt that gnaws at me as I sense how
    uncaring I have become.

Lord, grant me your grace …
Grace that will give new meaning and understanding of
    your purpose for my life.
Grace that will allow your love to flow more freely through
    me to others.

7-26-79

RENEWAL

My small inner voice kept saying, "Don't do it; don't do it." And I, with an overpowering urge to take my own direction, ignored the words that I somehow sensed were for the better good.

Now I am overcome with remorse. What is there within me that is at times so defiant to God's leading, so bent on having its own way?

I thank you, God, for the love and mercy that you offer us through your son, Jesus—grace that lifts me out of my distress and makes me more able to follow you in the days ahead.

7-29-79

ACCEPTANCE

Peter declared to him, "Though they all fall away because of you, I will never fall away." Jesus said to him, "Truly, I say to you, this very night, before the cock crows, you will deny me three times." Peter said to him, "Even if I must die with you, I will not deny you." And so said all the disciples.

—Matthew 26:33-35

I think I know how you felt, Peter, living those years with Jesus, secure in His love. And even though you sometimes stumbled, He was always close by with an open heart, offering His friendship.

I've heard your story again and again—how much you loved Him and how confident you were that no matter what happened, you would always be faithful. But then in those dark hours, it happened—the unrestrained denial. It must have erupted in an overwhelming surge of fear.

I have also seen His face, walked by His side in close communion, felt myself stronger for having known Him. Yet denial is a part of my life, just as it was a part of yours. At times, I am afraid to speak the truth because of the possible consequences. I close my eyes to conditions that challenge me to positive action, because my faith is weak.

Peter, I am thankful that I have the same Lord as you— one who knows my shortcomings and accepts me as I am, who reaches out in understanding and compassion to heal and renew.

Yes, I know how you felt.

7-29-79

The Indwelling Christ

Christ's resurrection is my resurrection. He comes into my life, bringing all that He is—dead, resurrected, ascended. And as this truth is lived out in me, the kingdom of Heaven opens wide its doors.

7-29-79

EASTER

Easter is a time of joy, expectation, and beauty. I see it in the glowing face of a happy young child or the warm embrace of two friends who have been apart too long. The delicate petals of the flower newly opened to the early morning sun tell me there is meaning in beauty. Hearts on fire with thankfulness are a witness to the blessings of Easter.

But there are other scenes that leave me baffled. Where is the joy of a heart broken over the loss of a loved one? How can there be beauty in long years of wearisome toil that bring forth few pleasures and little reward? Where is the expectation for a child being destroyed by hunger or a life that drags out beyond the time of good health and awareness?

If I am to know the true meaning of Easter, I must look beyond what I can see with my eyes. Somehow, in a way I do not really understand, I believe the answer is to be found in God's revelation in Jesus Christ—in His life, death, and resurrection. God has given us a gift—a sign of His all-encompassing love for His creation. Easter finds its meaning in the love that transcends all else.

7-27-79

STILLNESS

"Be still and know that I am God" (Psalm 46:10).

And with the knowing, the greater stillness comes.

9-25-79

QUIETNESS

For which quietness do I hunger?

It is not really the absence of outside disturbances, for even in such times, my mind is often exploding from the chaos of endless things crying out for my attention.

There is another stillness I seek—a kind of order that calmly meets each moment with the assurance that life is in the hands of a loving God who wants only the best for His children. In that secret, inner place where we meet, a quietness is born—a quietness that only God can bring.

9-22-79

A CUP OF WATER

He walks the bustling city streets …unknown, unnoticed, with a heart that aches for friendship and love.

In prison cells, He lives …His face masked with despair and hopelessness, crying out for someone to care.

He slowly dies of hunger …His body wasting away, too weak to protest the pain that reflects in hollow, pleading eyes.

He dwells with me …turning my heart to love, to care, to offer a cup of water in His name.

9-28-79

THE CHRIST

Who can capture Christ's image? Like ocean waves that defy the artist's brush with an ever-changing contour, He moves through our lives.

As thoughts begin to mold themselves to picture the Christ we know, He reveals Himself in some new way, and visions are expanded to receive more of a living Lord.

10-16-79

The Christ in All of Us

There is something of Christ in each of us. He waits for our hearts to open to release His love and compassion in ministry to others.

10-16-79

The Abiding One

The things that mean the most to us sooner or later must be released, for life has a way of moving on.

God must understand how much we need to cling to something permanent, for He offers Himself to us and comes to stay.

10-16-79

FORGIVENESS

With the gray days of winter behind her, nature bursts forth in a profusion of color, singing her song of joy with no sign of bitterness for the harshness that for a time despoiled her beauty.

Such forgiveness, total and unconditional, sweeps clean the path for love's expression.

8-80

VICTORY

After watching a TV show about Abraham Lincoln, I thought about his untimely and shocking death. Lincoln died, and everyone from his time in history is also dead. The trauma of death is related to its time; its impact is dependent on its place in time. But if we see ourselves released from this prison of time, living in another dimension as we live in time, does death have any impact? Is it really any threat?

Our life outside *time* is as real as our life encased in time, and if we allow ourselves to live within this freedom of spirit, even though we must continue our *time life* and have responsibility to it, we can see that the spirit is not defeated in death—that life does not cease with death. There is meaning in the *life beyond time*; it is a real life that can actually be experienced now in time if we will but open our minds, hearts, and very beings to such a possibility so it can be a part of our experience.

We see tragedy around us and are overcome with its oppression. But tragedy fades out in the reality of a spiritual life that is victorious, unending, eternal.

2-8-81

The Touch

I could never bring myself to approach the king. Awkwardness and indecision quickly dispelled any confidence I might have had to seek such an audience.

But when I saw the babe, my inhibitions faded. As the small, open hand reached out, my response was spontaneous. Our hands met, and we were one, simply by the touching.

As time passed, I would come to know this babe as King, but that could wait. For the moment, we would be babes together.

2-24-81

Printed in the United States
By Bookmasters